# HORN

# 101 BROADWAY SONGS

Note: The keys in this book do not match the other wind instruments.

Available for
FLUTE, CLARINET, ALTO SAX, TENOR SAX, TRUMPET,
HORN, TROMBONE, VIOLIN, VIOLA, CELLO

T8116612

ISBN 978-1-4950-5251-4

HAL•LEONARD® CORPORATION
7777 W. BLUEMOUND RD. P.O. BOX 13819 MILWAUKEE, WI 53213

For all works contained herein:
Unauthorized copying, arranging, adapting, recording, Internet posting, public performance, or other distribution of the printed music in this publication is an infringement of copyright. Infringers are liable under the law.

Visit Hal Leonard Online at
**www.halleonard.com**

# CONTENTS


4 All I Ask of You
5 Any Dream Will Do
6 Anything You Can Do
7 As If We Never Said Goodbye
8 As Long as He Needs Me
9 Bali Ha'i
10 Baubles, Bangles and Beads
11 Brotherhood of Man
12 Cabaret
13 Can't Take My Eyes Off of You
14 Circle of Life
15 Climb Ev'ry Mountain
16 Close Every Door
17 Dancing Queen
18 Defying Gravity
20 Do-Re-Mi
21 Do You Hear the People Sing?
22 Don't Cry for Me Argentina
23 Easter Parade
24 Edelweiss
25 Everything's Alright
26 A Foggy Day (In London Town)
28 Friend Like Me
27 Getting to Know You
30 Guys and Dolls
31 Hello, Dolly!
32 Home
34 How Are Things in Glocca Morra
35 I Believe in You
36 I Don't Know How to Love Him
37 I Dreamed a Dream
38 I Got Plenty o' Nuttin'
39 I Whistle a Happy Tune
40 I've Never Been in Love Before
41 If I Loved You
42 If I Were a Bell
43 If I Were a Rich Man
44 The Impossible Dream (The Quest)
45 It Ain't Necessarily So
46 The Lady Is a Tramp
47 The Last Night of the World
48 Let's Call the Whole Thing Off
49 Love Is Here to Stay
50 Love Me or Leave Me
51 Love Walked In
52 Luck Be a Lady
53 Makin' Whoopee!

54 Mame
55 Mamma Mia
56 Matchmaker
57 Maybe
58 Memory
59 The Music of the Night
60 My Favorite Things
61 Nice Work If You Can Get It
62 Oh, What a Beautiful Mornin'
63 Oklahoma
64 Ol' Man River
65 Old Devil Moon
66 On My Own
67 Once in a Lifetime
68 Once in Love with Amy
69 One
70 People Will Say We're in Love
71 The Phantom of the Opera
72 Popular
74 Seasons of Love
76 Send in the Clowns
77 Seventy Six Trombones
78 Shall We Dance?
79 She Loves Me
80 Sherry
81 Some Enchanted Evening
82 Summertime
83 Sunrise, Sunset
84 Superstar
85 The Surrey with the Fringe on Top
86 The Sweetest Sounds
87 There's No Business Like Show Business
88 They All Laughed
89 They Can't Take That Away from Me
90 Think of Me
91 This Is the Moment
92 This Nearly Was Mine
93 Till There Was You
94 Tomorrow
96 Unusual Way
95 Walk Like a Man
98 What I Did for Love
99 What Kind of Fool Am I?
100 Where Is Love?
101 Who Can I Turn To (When Nobody Needs Me)
102 A Whole New World
103 Will You Love Me Tomorrow (Will You Still Love Me Tomorrow)
104 With One Look
105 Written in the Stars
106 You Rule My World
108 You'll Be in My Heart
107 You'll Never Walk Alone
110 You've Got a Friend
112 Younger Than Springtime

# ALL I ASK OF YOU

from THE PHANTOM OF THE OPERA

HORN

Music by ANDREW LLOYD WEBBER
Lyrics by CHARLES HART
Additional Lyrics by RICHARD STILGOE

© Copyright 1986 Andrew Lloyd Webber licensed to The Really Useful Group Ltd.
International Copyright Secured All Rights Reserved

# ANY DREAM WILL DO

from JOSEPH AND THE AMAZING TECHNICOLOR® DREAMCOAT

HORN

Music by ANDREW LLOYD WEBBER
Lyrics by TIM RICE

© Copyright 1969 The Really Useful Group Ltd.
Copyright Renewed
International Copyright Secured All Rights Reserved

# ANYTHING YOU CAN DO

from the Stage Production ANNIE GET YOUR GUN

HORN

Words and Music by
IRVING BERLIN

© Copyright 1946 by Irving Berlin
Copyright Renewed
International Copyright Secured All Rights Reserved

# AS IF WE NEVER SAID GOODBYE

from SUNSET BOULEVARD

HORN

Music by ANDREW LLOYD WEBBER
Lyrics by DON BLACK and CHRISTOPHER HAMPTON,
with contributions by AMY POWERS

© Copyright 1993 Andrew Lloyd Webber licensed to The Really Useful Group Ltd.
International Copyright Secured All Rights Reserved

# AS LONG AS HE NEEDS ME

from the Broadway Musical OLIVER!

HORN

Words and Music by
LIONEL BART

© Copyright 1960 (Renewed) Lakeview Music Co., Ltd., London, England
TRO - Hollis Music, Inc., New York, controls all publication rights for the U.S.A. and Canada
International Copyright Secured
All Rights Reserved Including Public Performance For Profit
Used by Permission

# BALI HA'I

from SOUTH PACIFIC

HORN

Lyrics by OSCAR HAMMERSTEIN II
Music by RICHARD RODGERS

Copyright © 1949 by Richard Rodgers and Oscar Hammerstein II
Copyright Renewed
Williamson Music, a Division of Rodgers & Hammerstein: an Imagem Company, owner of publication and allied rights throughout the world
International Copyright Secured All Rights Reserved

# BAUBLES, BANGLES AND BEADS

from KISMET

HORN

Words and Music by ROBERT WRIGHT
and GEORGE FORREST
(Music Based on Themes of A. BORODIN)

Copyright © 1953 Frank Music Corp.
Copyright Renewed and Assigned to Scheffel Music Corp., New York, NY
All Rights Controlled by Scheffel Music Corp.
All Rights Reserved Used by Permission

# BROTHERHOOD OF MAN

from HOW TO SUCCEED IN BUSINESS WITHOUT REALLY TRYING

HORN

By FRANK LOESSER

© 1961 (Renewed) FRANK MUSIC CORP.
All Rights Reserved

# CABARET

from the Musical CABARET

HORN

Words by FRED EBB
Music by JOHN KANDER

Copyright © 1966, 1967 by Alley Music Corp. and Trio Music Company
Copyright Renewed
All Rights for Trio Music Company Administered by BMG Rights Management (US) LLC
International Copyright Secured All Rights Reserved
Used by Permission

# CAN'T TAKE MY EYES OFF OF YOU

featured in JERSEY BOYS

HORN

Words and Music by BOB CREWE
and BOB GAUDIO

Copyright © 1967 EMI Longitude Music and Seasons Four Music
Copyright Renewed
All Rights on behalf of EMI Longitude Music Administered by Sony/ATV Music Publishing LLC, 424 Church Street, Suite 1200, Nashville, TN 37219
International Copyright Secured All Rights Reserved

# CIRCLE OF LIFE

Disney Presents THE LION KING: THE BROADWAY MUSICAL

HORN

Music by ELTON JOHN
Lyrics by TIM RICE

**Moderately, with an African beat**

© 1994 Wonderland Music Company, Inc.
All Rights Reserved Used by Permission

# CLIMB EV'RY MOUNTAIN

from THE SOUND OF MUSIC

HORN

Lyrics by OSCAR HAMMERSTEIN II
Music by RICHARD RODGERS

Copyright © 1959 by Richard Rodgers and Oscar Hammerstein II
Copyright Renewed
Williamson Music, a Division of Rodgers & Hammerstein: an Imagem Company, owner of publication and allied rights throughout the world
International Copyright Secured All Rights Reserved

# CLOSE EVERY DOOR

from JOSEPH AND THE AMAZING TECHNICOLOR® DREAMCOAT

HORN

Music by ANDREW LLOYD WEBBER
Lyrics by TIM RICE

**Moderately, expressively**

© Copyright 1969 The Really Useful Group Ltd.
Copyright Renewed
International Copyright Secured All Rights Reserved

# DANCING QUEEN

from MAMMA MIA!

HORN

Words and Music by BENNY ANDERSSON,
BJÖRN ULVAEUS and STIG ANDERSON

Copyright © 1977 UNIVERSAL/UNION SONGS MUSIKFORLAG AB
Copyright Renewed
All Rights in the United States and Canada Controlled and Administered by
UNIVERSAL - SONGS OF POLYGRAM INTERNATIONAL, INC. and EMI GROVE PARK MUSIC, INC.
All Rights Reserved Used by Permission

# DEFYING GRAVITY

from the Broadway Musical WICKED

HORN

Music and Lyrics by
STEPHEN SCHWARTZ

Copyright © 2003 Grey Dog Music
All Rights Reserved Used by Permission

Tempo I

# DO-RE-MI

from THE SOUND OF MUSIC

HORN

Lyrics by OSCAR HAMMERSTEIN II
Music by RICHARD RODGERS

Copyright © 1959 by Richard Rodgers and Oscar Hammerstein II
Copyright Renewed
Williamson Music, a Division of Rodgers & Hammerstein: an Imagem Company, owner of publication and allied rights throughout the world
International Copyright Secured All Rights Reserved

# DO YOU HEAR THE PEOPLE SING?

from LES MISÉRABLES

HORN

Music by CLAUDE-MICHEL SCHÖNBERG
Lyrics by ALAIN BOUBLIL, JEAN-MARC NATEL
and HERBERT KRETZMER

**March tempo**

Music and Lyrics Copyright © 1980 by Editions Musicales Alain Boublil
English Lyrics Copyright © 1986 by Alain Boublil Music Ltd. (ASCAP)
Mechanical and Publication Rights for the U.S.A. Administered by Alain Boublil Music Ltd. (ASCAP) c/o Joel Faden & Co., Inc.,
MLM 250 West 57th St., 26th Floor, New York, NY 10107, Tel. (212) 246-7203, Fax (212) 246-7217, jfaden@joelfaden.com
International Copyright Secured. All Rights Reserved. This music is copyright. Photocopying is illegal.
All Performance Rights Restricted.

# DON'T CRY FOR ME ARGENTINA

from EVITA

HORN

Words by TIM RICE
Music by ANDREW LLOYD WEBBER

Copyright © 1976, 1977 EVITA MUSIC LTD.
Copyright Renewed
All Rights for the United States and Canada Controlled and Administered by UNIVERSAL MUSIC CORP.
All Rights Reserved Used by Permission

# EASTER PARADE

from AS THOUSANDS CHEER

HORN

Words and Music by
IRVING BERLIN

© Copyright 1933 by Irving Berlin
Copyright Renewed
International Copyright Secured All Rights Reserved

# EDELWEISS

from THE SOUND OF MUSIC

HORN

Lyrics by OSCAR HAMMERSTEIN II
Music by RICHARD RODGERS

**Slowly, with expression**

Copyright © 1959 by Richard Rodgers and Oscar Hammerstein II
Copyright Renewed
Williamson Music, a Division of Rodgers & Hammerstein: an Imagem Company, owner of publication and allied rights throughout the world
International Copyright Secured All Rights Reserved

# EVERYTHING'S ALRIGHT

from JESUS CHRIST SUPERSTAR

HORN

Words by TIM RICE
Music by ANDREW LLOYD WEBBER

Copyright © 1970, 1971 UNIVERSAL / MCA MUSIC LTD.
Copyrights Renewed
All Rights for the U.S. and Canada Controlled and Administered by UNIVERSAL MUSIC CORP.
All Rights Reserved Used by Permission

# A FOGGY DAY (IN LONDON TOWN)

from A DAMSEL IN DISTRESS

HORN

Music and Lyrics by GEORGE GERSHWIN
and IRA GERSHWIN

© 1937 (Renewed) NOKAWI MUSIC, FRANKIE G. SONGS and IRA GERSHWIN MUSIC
All Rights for NOKAWI MUSIC Administered by IMAGEM SOUNDS
All Rights for FRANKIE G. SONGS Administered by SONGS MUSIC PUBLISHING
All Rights for IRA GERSHWIN MUSIC Administered by WB MUSIC CORP.
All Rights Reserved Used by Permission

# GETTING TO KNOW YOU

from THE KING AND I

HORN

Lyrics by OSCAR HAMMERSTEIN II
Music by RICHARD RODGERS

Copyright © 1951 by Richard Rodgers and Oscar Hammerstein II
Copyright Renewed
Williamson Music, a Division of Rodgers & Hammerstein: an Imagem Company, owner of publication and allied rights throughout the world
International Copyright Secured All Rights Reserved

# FRIEND LIKE ME

(Stageplay Version)

from the Walt Disney Stageplay ALADDIN

HORN

Music by ALAN MENKEN
Lyrics by HOWARD ASHMAN
and STEPHEN SCHWARTZ

© 2014 Walt Disney Music Company and Wonderland Music Company, Inc.
All Rights Reserved Used by Permission

# GUYS AND DOLLS

from GUYS AND DOLLS

HORN

By FRANK LOESSER

© 1950 (Renewed) FRANK MUSIC CORP.
All Rights Reserved

# HELLO, DOLLY!

from HELLO, DOLLY!

HORN

Music and Lyric by
JERRY HERMAN

© 1963 (Renewed) JERRY HERMAN
All Rights Controlled by EDWIN H. MORRIS & COMPANY, A Division of MPL Music Publishing, Inc.
All Rights Reserved

# HOME

from Walt Disney's BEAUTY AND THE BEAST: THE BROADWAY MUSICAL

HORN

Music by ALAN MENKEN
Lyrics by TIM RICE

© 1994 Wonderland Music Company, Inc., Menken Music, Trunksong Music Ltd. and Walt Disney Music Company
All Rights Reserved Used by Permission

1.
2.

# HOW ARE THINGS IN GLOCCA MORRA

from FINIAN'S RAINBOW

HORN

Words by E.Y. "YIP" HARBURG
Music by BURTON LANE

Copyright © 1946 by Chappell & Co., Inc. and Glocca Morra Music
Copyright Renewed
All Rights for Glocca Morra Music Administered by Shapiro, Bernstein & Co., Inc., New York
International Copyright Secured All Rights Reserved

# I BELIEVE IN YOU

from HOW TO SUCCEED IN BUSINESS WITHOUT REALLY TRYING

HORN

By FRANK LOESSER

© 1961 (Renewed) FRANK MUSIC CORP.
All Rights Reserved

# I DON'T KNOW HOW TO LOVE HIM

from JESUS CHRIST SUPERSTAR

HORN

Words by TIM RICE
Music by ANDREW LLOYD WEBBER

Copyright © 1971 UNIVERSAL / MCA MUSIC LTD.
Copyright Renewed
All Rights for the U.S. and Canada Controlled and Administered by UNIVERSAL MUSIC CORP.
All Rights Reserved Used by Permission

# I DREAMED A DREAM

from LES MISÉRABLES

HORN

Music by CLAUDE-MICHEL SCHÖNBERG
Lyrics by ALAIN BOUBLIL, JEAN-MARC NATEL
and HERBERT KRETZMER

Music and Lyrics Copyright © 1980 by Editions Musicales Alain Boublil
English Lyrics Copyright © 1986 by Alain Boublil Music Ltd. (ASCAP)
Mechanical and Publication Rights for the U.S.A. Administered by Alain Boublil Music Ltd. (ASCAP) c/o Joel Faden & Co., Inc.,
MLM 250 West 57th St., 26th Floor, New York, NY 10107, Tel. (212) 246-7203, Fax (212) 246-7217, jfaden@joelfaden.com
International Copyright Secured. All Rights Reserved. This music is copyright. Photocopying is illegal.
All Performance Rights Restricted.

# I GOT PLENTY O' NUTTIN'

from PORGY AND BESS®

HORN

Music and Lyrics by GEORGE GERSHWIN,
DuBOSE and DORTHY HEYWARD
and IRA GERSHWIN

© 1935 (Renewed) NOKAWI MUSIC, FRANKIE G. SONGS, DuBOSE AND DOROTHY HEYWARD MEMORIAL FUND PUBLISHING and IRA GERSHWIN MUSIC
All Rights for NOKAWI MUSIC Administered by IMAGEM SOUNDS
All Rights for FRANKIE G. SONGS and DuBOSE AND DOROTHY HEYWARD MEMORIAL FUND PUBLISHING Administered by SONGS MUSIC PUBLISHING
All Rights for IRA GERSHWIN MUSIC Administered by WB MUSIC CORP.
All Rights Reserved Used by Permission

# I WHISTLE A HAPPY TUNE

from THE KING AND I

HORN

Lyrics by OSCAR HAMMERSTEIN II
Music by RICHARD RODGERS

Copyright © 1951 by Richard Rodgers and Oscar Hammerstein II
Copyright Renewed
Williamson Music, a Division of Rodgers & Hammerstein: an Imagem Company, owner of publication and allied rights throughout the world
International Copyright Secured All Rights Reserved

# I'VE NEVER BEEN IN LOVE BEFORE

from GUYS AND DOLLS

HORN

By FRANK LOESSER

© 1950 (Renewed) FRANK MUSIC CORP.
All Rights Reserved

# IF I LOVED YOU

from CAROUSEL

HORN

Lyrics by OSCAR HAMMERSTEIN II
Music by RICHARD RODGERS

Copyright © 1945 by Williamson Music, a Division of Rodgers & Hammerstein: an Imagem Company
Copyright Renewed
International Copyright Secured All Rights Reserved

# IF I WERE A BELL

from GUYS AND DOLLS

HORN

By FRANK LOESSER

© 1950 (Renewed) FRANK MUSIC CORP.
All Rights Reserved

# IF I WERE A RICH MAN

from the Musical FIDDLER ON THE ROOF

HORN

Words by SHELDON HARNICK
Music by JERRY BOCK

Copyright © 1964 Bock IP LLC and Mayerling Productions, Ltd.
Copyright Renewed 1992
All Rights for Mayerling Productions, Ltd. Administered by R&H Music, a Division of Rodgers & Hammerstein: an Imagem Company
International Copyright Secured All Rights Reserved

# THE IMPOSSIBLE DREAM

(The Quest)

from MAN OF LA MANCHA

HORN

Lyric by JOE DARION
Music by MITCH LEIGH

Copyright © 1965 (Renewed 1994) Andrew Scott, Inc. and Helena Music Corp.
International Copyright Secured All Rights Reserved

# IT AIN'T NECESSARILY SO

from PORGY AND BESS®

HORN

Music and Lyrics by GEORGE GERSHWIN,
DuBOSE and DOROTHY HEYWARD
and IRA GERSHWIN

© 1935 (Renewed) NOKAWI MUSIC, FRANKIE G. SONGS, DuBOSE AND DOROTHY HEYWARD MEMORIAL FUND PUBLISHING and IRA GERSHWIN MUSIC
All Rights for NOKAWI MUSIC Administered by IMAGEM SOUNDS
All Rights for FRANKIE G. SONGS and DuBOSE AND DOROTHY HEYWARD MEMORIAL FUND PUBLISHING Administered by SONGS MUSIC PUBLISHING
All Rights for IRA GERSHWIN MUSIC Administered by WB MUSIC CORP.
All Rights Reserved Used by Permission

# THE LADY IS A TRAMP

from BABES IN ARMS

HORN

Words by LORENZ HART
Music by RICHARD RODGERS

Copyright © 1937 by Chappell & Co.
Copyright Renewed and Assigned to Imagem CV and WB Music Corp. for the United States and British Reversionary Territories
International Copyright Secured All Rights Reserved

# THE LAST NIGHT OF THE WORLD

from MISS SAIGON

HORN

Music by CLAUDE-MICHEL SCHÖNBERG
Lyrics by RICHARD MALTBY JR. and ALAIN BOUBLIL
Adapted from original French Lyrics by ALAIN BOUBLIL

**Languidly**

Music and Lyrics Copyright © 1987 by Alain Boublil Music Ltd. (ASCAP)
English Lyrics Copyright © 1988 by Alain Boublil Music Ltd. (ASCAP)
Additional Music and English Lyrics Copyright © 1989 and 1991 by Alain Boublil Music Ltd. (ASCAP)
Mechanical and Publication Rights for the U.S.A. Administered by Alain Boublil Music Ltd. (ASCAP) c/o Joel Faden & Co., Inc.,
MLM 250 West 57th St., 26th Floor, New York, NY 10107, Tel. (212) 246-7203, Fax (212) 246-7217, jfaden@joelfaden.com
International Copyright Secured. All Rights Reserved. This music is copyright. Photocopying is illegal.
All Performance Rights Restricted.

# LET'S CALL THE WHOLE THING OFF

from SHALL WE DANCE

HORN

Music and Lyrics by GEORGE GERSHWIN
and IRA GERSHWIN

© 1936 (Renewed) NOKAWI MUSIC, FRANKIE G. SONGS and IRA GERSHWIN MUSIC
All Rights for NOKAWI MUSIC Administered by IMAGEM SOUNDS
All Rights for FRANKIE G. SONGS Administered by SONGS MUSIC PUBLISHING
All Rights for IRA GERSHWIN MUSIC Administered by WB MUSIC CORP.
All Rights Reserved Used by Permission

# LOVE IS HERE TO STAY

from GOLDWYN FOLLIES

HORN

Music and Lyrics by GEORGE GERSHWIN
and IRA GERSHWIN

**Medium Swing** (♫ = ♩ 3 ♪)

© 1938 (Renewed) NOKAWI MUSIC, FRANKIE G. SONGS and IRA GERSHWIN MUSIC
All Rights for NOKAWI MUSIC Administered by IMAGEM SOUNDS
All Rights for FRANKIE G. SONGS Administered by SONGS MUSIC PUBLISHING
All Rights for IRA GERSHWIN MUSIC Administered by WB MUSIC CORP.
All Rights Reserved Used by Permission

# LOVE ME OR LEAVE ME

from WHOOPEE!

HORN

Lyrics by GUS KAHN
Music by WALTER DONALDSON

Copyright © 1928 (Renewed) by Donaldson Publishing Co., Dreyer Music Co. and Gilbert Keyes Music Co.
All Rights for Dreyer Music Co. Administered by Larry Spier, Inc., New York
All Rights for Gilbert Keyes Music Co. Administered by WB Music Corp.
International Copyright Secured All Rights Reserved

# LOVE WALKED IN

from GOLDWYN FOLLIES

HORN

Music and Lyrics by GEORGE GERSHWIN
and IRA GERSHWIN

© 1937, 1938 (Copyrights Renewed) NOKAWI MUSIC, FRANKIE G. SONGS and IRA GERSHWIN MUSIC
All Rights for NOKAWI MUSIC Administered by IMAGEM SOUNDS
All Rights for FRANKIE G. SONGS Administered by SONGS MUSIC PUBLISHING
All Rights for IRA GERSHWIN MUSIC Administered by WB MUSIC CORP.
All Rights Reserved Used by Permission

# LUCK BE A LADY

from GUYS AND DOLLS

HORN

By FRANK LOESSER

© 1950 (Renewed) FRANK MUSIC CORP.
All Rights Reserved

# MAKIN' WHOOPEE!

from WHOOPEE!

HORN

Lyrics by GUS KAHN
Music by WALTER DONALDSON

Copyright © 1928 (Renewed) by Donaldson Publishing Co., Dreyer Music Co. and Gilbert Keyes Music Company
All Rights for Dreyer Music Co. Administered by Larry Spier, Inc., New York
All Rights for Gilbert Keyes Music Company Administered by WB Music Corp.
International Copyright Secured All Rights Reserved

# MAME

from MAME

HORN

Music and Lyric by
JERRY HERMAN

**Medium Swing** (♫ = ♩ ♪)

© 1966 (Renewed) JERRY HERMAN
All Rights Controlled by JERRYCO MUSIC CO.
Exclusive Agent: EDWIN H. MORRIS & COMPANY, A Division of MPL Music Publishing, Inc.
All Rights Reserved

# MAMMA MIA

from MAMMA MIA!

HORN

Words and Music by BENNY ANDERSSON,
BJÖRN ULVAEUS and STIG ANDERSON

Copyright © 1975 UNIVERSAL/UNION SONGS MUSIKFORLAG AB
Copyright Renewed
All Rights in the United States and Canada Controlled and Administered by
UNIVERSAL - SONGS OF POLYGRAM INTERNATIONAL, INC. and EMI GROVE PARK MUSIC, INC.
Exclusive Print Rights for EMI GROVE PARK MUSIC, INC. Administered by ALFRED MUSIC
All Rights for UK/Eire Administered by BOCU MUSIC LTD.
All Rights Reserved Used by Permission

# MATCHMAKER

from the Musical FIDDLER ON THE ROOF

HORN

Words by SHELDON HARNICK
Music by JERRY BOCK

Copyright © 1964 Bock IP LLC and Mayerling Productions, Ltd.
Copyright Renewed 1992
All Rights for Mayerling Productions, Ltd. Administered by R&H Music, a Division of Rodgers & Hammerstein: an Imagem Company
International Copyright Secured All Rights Reserved

# MAYBE

from the Musical Production ANNIE

HORN

Lyric by MARTIN CHARNIN
Music by CHARLES STROUSE

© 1977 (Renewed) EDWIN H. MORRIS & COMPANY, A Division of MPL Music Publishing, Inc. and CHARLES STROUSE PUBLISHING
All Rights for CHARLES STROUSE PUBLISHING Administered by WB MUSIC CORP.
All Rights Reserved Used by Permission

# MEMORY

from CATS

HORN

Music by ANDREW LLOYD WEBBER
Text by TREVOR NUNN after T.S. ELIOT

Music Copyright © 1981 Andrew Lloyd Webber licensed to The Really Useful Group Ltd.
Text Copyright © 1981 Trevor Nunn and Set Copyrights Ltd.
All Rights in the text Controlled by Faber and Faber Ltd. and Administered for the United States and Canada by
R&H Music Co., a Division of Rodgers & Hammerstein: an Imagem Company
International Copyright Secured All Rights Reserved

# THE MUSIC OF THE NIGHT

from THE PHANTOM OF THE OPERA

HORN

Music by ANDREW LLOYD WEBBER
Lyrics by CHARLES HART
Additional Lyrics by RICHARD STILGOE

© Copyright 1986 Andrew Lloyd Webber licensed to The Really Useful Group Ltd.
International Copyright Secured All Rights Reserved

# MY FAVORITE THINGS

from THE SOUND OF MUSIC

HORN

Lyrics by OSCAR HAMMERSTEIN II
Music by RICHARD RODGERS

Copyright © 1959 by Richard Rodgers and Oscar Hammerstein II
Copyright Renewed
Williamson Music, a Division of Rodgers & Hammerstein: an Imagem Company, owner of publication and allied rights throughout the world
International Copyright Secured All Rights Reserved

# NICE WORK IF YOU CAN GET IT

from A DAMSEL IN DISTRESS

HORN

Music and Lyrics by GEORGE GERSHWIN
and IRA GERSWIN

© 1937 (Renewed) NOKAWI MUSIC, FRANKIE G. SONGS and IRA GERSHWIN MUSIC
All Rights for NOKAWI MUSIC Administered by IMAGEM SOUNDS
All Rights for FRANKIE G. SONGS Administered by SONGS MUSIC PUBLISHING
All Rights for IRA GERSHWIN MUSIC Administered by WB MUSIC CORP.
All Rights Reserved Used by Permission

# OH, WHAT A BEAUTIFUL MORNIN'

from OKLAHOMA!

HORN

Lyrics by OSCAR HAMMERSTEIN II
Music by RICHARD RODGERS

**Bright Waltz**

Copyright © 1943 by Williamson Music, a Division of Rodgers & Hammerstein: an Imagem Company
Copyright Renewed
International Copyright Secured All Rights Reserved

# OKLAHOMA

from OKLAHOMA!

HORN

Lyrics by OSCAR HAMMERSTEIN II
Music by RICHARD RODGERS

Copyright © 1943 by Williamson Music, a Division of Rodgers & Hammerstein: an Imagem Company
Copyright Renewed
International Copyright Secured All Rights Reserved

# OL' MAN RIVER

from SHOW BOAT

HORN

Lyrics by OSCAR HAMMERSTEIN II
Music by JEROME KERN

Copyright © 1927 UNIVERSAL - POLYGRAM INTERNATIONAL PUBLISHING, INC.
Copyright Renewed
All Rights Reserved Used by Permission

# OLD DEVIL MOON

from FINIAN'S RAINBOW

HORN

Words by E.Y. "YIP" HARBURG
Music by BURTON LANE

Copyright © 1946 by Chappell & Co., Inc. and Glocca Morra Music
Copyright Renewed
All Rights for Glocca Morra Music Administered by Shapiro, Bernstein & Co., Inc.
International Copyright Secured All Rights Reserved

# ON MY OWN

from LES MISÉRABLES

HORN

Music by CLAUDE-MICHEL SCHÖNBERG
Lyrics by ALAIN BOUBLIL, JEAN-MARC NATEL,
HERBERT KRETZMER, JOHN CAIRD
and TREVOR NUNN

**Moderately slow**

Music and Lyrics Copyright © 1980 by Editions Musicales Alain Boublil
English Lyrics Copyright © 1986 by Alain Boublil Music Ltd. (ASCAP)
Mechanical and Publication Rights for the U.S.A. Administered by Alain Boublil Music Ltd. (ASCAP) c/o Joel Faden & Co., Inc.,
MLM 250 West 57th St., 26th Floor, New York, NY 10107, Tel. (212) 246-7203, Fax (212) 246-7217, jfaden@joelfaden.com
International Copyright Secured. All Rights Reserved. This music is copyright. Photocopying is illegal.
All Performance Rights Restricted.

# ONCE IN A LIFETIME

from the Musical Production STOP THE WORLD—I WANT TO GET OFF

HORN

Words and Music by LESLIE BRICUSSE
and ANTHONY NEWLEY

© Copyright 1961 (Renewed) TRO Essex Music Ltd., London, England
TRO - Ludlow Music, Inc., New York, controls all publication rights for the U.S.A. and Canada
International Copyright Secured
All Rights Reserved Including Public Performance For Profit
Used by Permission

# ONCE IN LOVE WITH AMY

from WHERE'S CHARLEY?

HORN

By FRANK LOESSER

© 1948 (Renewed) FRANK MUSIC CORP.
All Rights Reserved

# ONE

from A CHORUS LINE

HORN

Music by MARVIN HAMLISCH
Lyric by EDWARD KLEBAN

© 1975 (Renewed) EDWARD KLEBAN and SONY/ATV MUSIC PUBLISHING LLC
All Rights for EDWARD KLEBAN Controlled by WREN MUSIC CO.
All Rights for SONY/ATV MUSIC PUBLISHING LLC Administered by SONY/ATV MUSIC PUBLISHING LLC, 424 Church Street, Suite 1200, Nashville, TN 37219
All Rights Reserved

# PEOPLE WILL SAY WE'RE IN LOVE

from OKLAHOMA!

HORN

Lyrics by OSCAR HAMMERSTEIN II
Music by RICHARD RODGERS

Copyright © 1943 by Williamson Music, a Division of Rodgers & Hammerstein: an Imagem Company
Copyright Renewed
International Copyright Secured All Rights Reserved

# THE PHANTOM OF THE OPERA

from THE PHANTOM OF THE OPERA

HORN

Music by ANDREW LLOYD WEBBER
Lyrics by CHARLES HART
Additional Lyrics by RICHARD STILGOE
and MIKE BATT

© Copyright 1986 Andrew Lloyd Webber licensed to The Really Useful Group Ltd.
International Copyright Secured All Rights Reserved

# POPULAR

from the Broadway Musical WICKED

HORN

Music and Lyrics by
STEPHEN SCHWARTZ

Copyright © 2003 Grey Dog Music
All Rights Reserved Used by Permission

# SEASONS OF LOVE

from RENT

HORN

Words and Music by
JONATHAN LARSON

Copyright © 1996 FINSTER & LUCY MUSIC LTD. CO.
All Rights Controlled and Administered by UNIVERSAL MUSIC CORP.
All Rights Reserved Used by Permission

# SEND IN THE CLOWNS

from the Musical A LITTLE NIGHT MUSIC

HORN

Words and Music by
STEPHEN SONDHEIM

© 1973 (Renewed) RILTING MUSIC, INC.
All Rights Administered by WB MUSIC CORP.
All Rights Reserved Used by Permission

# SEVENTY SIX TROMBONES

from Meredith Willson's THE MUSIC MAN

HORN

By MEREDITH WILLSON

© 1957 (Renewed) FRANK MUSIC CORP. and MEREDITH WILLSON MUSIC
All Rights Reserved

# SHALL WE DANCE?

from THE KING AND I

HORN

Lyrics by OSCAR HAMMERSTEIN II
Music by RICHARD RODGERS

Copyright © 1951 by Richard Rodgers and Oscar Hammerstein II
Copyright Renewed
Williamson Music, a Division of Rodgers & Hammerstein: an Imagem Company, owner of publication and allied rights throughout the world
International Copyright Secured All Rights Reserved

# SHE LOVES ME

from SHE LOVES ME

HORN

Words by SHELDON HARNICK
Music by JERRY BOCK

Copyright © 1963 Bock IP LLC and Mayerling Productions, Ltd.
Copyright Renewed 1991
All Rights for Mayerling Productions, Ltd. Administered by R&H Music, a Division of Rodgers & Hammerstein: an Imagem Company
International Copyright Secured All Rights Reserved

# SHERRY

featured in JERSEY BOYS

HORN

Words and Music by
BOB GAUDIO

© 1962, 1963 (Renewed) CLARIDGE MUSIC COMPANY, A Division of MPL Music Publishing, Inc.
All Rights Reserved

# SOME ENCHANTED EVENING

from SOUTH PACIFIC

HORN

Lyrics by OSCAR HAMMERSTEIN II
Music by RICHARD RODGERS

Copyright © 1949 by Richard Rodgers and Oscar Hammerstein II
Copyright Renewed
Williamson Music, a Division of Rodgers & Hammerstein: an Imagem Company, owner of publication and allied rights throughout the world
International Copyright Secured All Rights Reserved

# SUMMERTIME

from PORGY AND BESS®

HORN

Music and Lyrics by GEORGE GERSHWIN,
DuBOSE and DOROTHY HEYWARD
and IRA GERSHWIN

© 1935 (Renewed) NOKAWI MUSIC, FRANKIE G. SONGS, DuBOSE AND DOROTHY HEYWARD MEMORIAL FUND PUBLISHING and IRA GERSHWIN MUSIC
All Rights for NOKAWI MUSIC Administered by IMAGEM SOUNDS
All Rights for FRANKIE G. SONGS and DuBOSE AND DOROTHY HEYWARD MEMORIAL FUND PUBLISHING Administered by SONGS MUSIC PUBLISHING
All Rights for IRA GERSHWIN MUSIC Administered by WB MUSIC CORP.
All Rights Reserved Used by Permission

# SUNRISE, SUNSET

from the Musical FIDDLER ON THE ROOF

HORN

Words by SHELDON HARNICK
Music by JERRY BOCK

**Moderately slow Waltz**

Copyright © 1964 Bock IP LLC and Mayerling Productions, Ltd.
Copyright Renewed 1992
All Rights for Mayerling Productions, Ltd. Administered by R&H Music, a Division of Rodgers & Hammerstein: an Imagem Company
International Copyright Secured All Rights Reserved

# SUPERSTAR

from JESUS CHRIST SUPERSTAR

HORN

Words by TIM RICE
Music by ANDREW LLOYD WEBBER

Copyright © 1969, 1970 UNIVERSAL / MCA MUSIC LTD.
Copyrights Renewed
All Rights for the U.S. and Canada Controlled and Administered by UNIVERSAL MUSIC CORP.
All Rights Reserved Used by Permission

# THE SURREY WITH THE FRINGE ON TOP

from OKLAHOMA!

HORN

Lyrics by OSCAR HAMMERSTEIN II
Music by RICHARD RODGERS

Copyright © 1943 by Williamson Music, a Division of Rodgers & Hammerstein: an Imagem Company
Copyright Renewed
International Copyright Secured All Rights Reserved

# THE SWEETEST SOUNDS

from NO STRINGS

HORN

Lyrics and Music by
RICHARD RODGERS

Copyright © 1962 by Richard Rodgers
Copyright Renewed
Williamson Music, a Division of Rodgers & Hammerstein: an Imagem Company, owner of publication and allied rights throughout the world
International Copyright Secured All Rights Reserved

# THERE'S NO BUSINESS LIKE SHOW BUSINESS

from the Stage Production ANNIE GET YOUR GUN

HORN

Words and Music by
IRVING BERLIN

© Copyright 1946 by Irving Berlin
Copyright Renewed
International Copyright Secured All Rights Reserved

# THEY ALL LAUGHED

from SHALL WE DANCE

HORN

Music and Lyrics by GEORGE GERSHWIN
and IRA GERSHWIN

© 1936 (Renewed) NOKAWI MUSIC, FRANKIE G. SONGS and IRA GERSHWIN MUSIC
All Rights for NOKAWI MUSIC Administered by IMAGEM SOUNDS
All Rights for FRANKIE G. SONGS Administered by SONGS MUSIC PUBLISHING
All Rights for IRA GERSHWIN MUSIC Administered by WB MUSIC CORP.
All Rights Reserved Used by Permission

# THEY CAN'T TAKE THAT AWAY FROM ME

from SHALL WE DANCE

HORN

Music and Lyrics by GEORGE GERSHWIN
and IRA GERSHWIN

© 1936 (Renewed) NOKAWI MUSIC, FRANKIE G. SONGS and IRA GERSHWIN MUSIC
All Rights for NOKAWI MUSIC Administered by IMAGEM SOUNDS
All Rights for FRANKIE G. SONGS Administered by SONGS MUSIC PUBLISHING
All Rights for IRA GERSHWIN MUSIC Administered by WB MUSIC CORP.
All Rights Reserved Used by Permission

# THINK OF ME

from THE PHANTOM OF THE OPERA

HORN

Music by ANDREW LLOYD WEBBER
Lyrics by CHARLES HART
Additional Lyrics by RICHARD STILGOE

© Copyright 1986 Andrew Lloyd Webber licensed to The Really Useful Group Ltd.
International Copyright Secured All Rights Reserved

# THIS IS THE MOMENT

from JEKYLL & HYDE

HORN

Words and Music by LESLIE BRICUSSE
and FRANK WILDHORN

Copyright © 1990, 1995, 1997 Painted Desert Music Corp. on behalf of Stage And Screen Music Inc., BMG Ruby Songs, Scaramanga Music, Inc. and Reservoir Media Music
All Rights for BMG Ruby Songs and Scaramanga Music, Inc. Administered by BMG Rights Management (US) LLC
All Rights for Reservoir Media Music Administered by Reservoir Media Management, Inc.
Reservoir Media Music Administered by Alfred Music
International Copyright Secured All Rights Reserved
Used by Permission

# THIS NEARLY WAS MINE

from SOUTH PACIFIC

HORN

Lyrics by OSCAR HAMMERSTEIN II
Music by RICHARD RODGERS

Copyright © 1949 by Richard Rodgers and Oscar Hammerstein II
Copyright Renewed
Williamson Music, a Division of Rodgers & Hammerstein: an Imagem Company, owner of publication and allied rights throughout the world
International Copyright Secured All Rights Reserved

# TILL THERE WAS YOU

from Meredith Willson's THE MUSIC MAN

HORN

By MEREDITH WILLSON

© 1950, 1957 (Renewed) FRANK MUSIC CORP. and MEREDITH WILLSON MUSIC
All Rights Reserved

# TOMORROW

from the Musical Production ANNIE

HORN

Lyric by MARTIN CHARNIN
Music by CHARLES STROUSE

© 1977 (Renewed) EDWIN H. MORRIS & COMPANY, A Division of MPL Music Publishing, Inc. and CHARLES STROUSE PUBLISHING
All Rights for CHARLES STROUSE PUBLISHING Administered by WB MUSIC CORP.
All Rights Reserved Used by Permission

# WALK LIKE A MAN

featured in JERSEY BOYS

HORN

Words and Music by BOB CREWE
and BOB GAUDIO

© 1963 (Renewed) CLARIDGE MUSIC COMPANY, A Division of MPL Music Publishing, Inc.
All Rights Reserved

# UNUSUAL WAY

from NINE

HORN

Music and Lyrics by
MAURY YESTON

Copyright © 1982 Yeston Music Ltd. (BMI)
All Rights Administered by BMG Rights Management (US) LLC
International Copyright Secured All Rights Reserved

3
3

# WHAT I DID FOR LOVE

from A CHORUS LINE

HORN

Music by MARVIN HAMLISCH
Lyric by EDWARD KLEBAN

© 1975 (Renewed) EDWARD KLEBAN and SONY/ATV MUSIC PUBLISHING LLC
All Rights for EDWARD KLEBAN Controlled by WREN MUSIC CO.
All Rights for SONY/ATV MUSIC PUBLISHING LLC Administered by SONY/ATV MUSIC PUBLISHING LLC, 424 Church Street, Suite 1200, Nashville, TN 37219'
All Rights Reserved

# WHAT KIND OF FOOL AM I?

from the Musical Production STOP THE WORLD—I WANT TO GET OFF

HORN

Words and Music by LESLIE BRICUSSE
and ANTHONY NEWLEY

© Copyright 1961 (Renewed) TRO Essex Music Ltd., London, England
TRO - Ludlow Music, Inc., New York, controls all publication rights for the U.S.A. and Canada
International Copyright Secured
All Rights Reserved Including Public Performance For Profit
Used by Permission

# WHERE IS LOVE?

from the Broadway Musical OLIVER!

HORN

Words and Music by
LIONEL BART

© Copyright 1960 (Renewed), 1968 (Renewed) Lakeview Music Co., Ltd., London, England
TRO - Hollis Music, Inc., New York, controls all publication rights for the U.S.A. and Canada
International Copyright Secured
All Rights Reserved Including Public Performance For Profit
Used by Permission

# WHO CAN I TURN TO

## (When Nobody Needs Me)

HORN

from THE ROAR OF THE GREASEPAINT—THE SMELL OF THE CROWD

Words and Music by LESLIE BRICUSSE
and ANTHONY NEWLEY

© Copyright 1964 (Renewed) Concord Music Ltd., London, England
TRO - Musical Comedy Productions, Inc., New York, controls all publication rights for the U.S.A. and Canada
International Copyright Secured
All Rights Reserved Including Public Performance For Profit
Used by Permission

# A WHOLE NEW WORLD

from the Walt Disney Stageplay ALADDIN

HORN

Music by ALAN MENKEN
Lyrics by TIM RICE

© 1992 Wonderland Music Company, Inc. and Walt Disney Music Company
All Rights Reserved Used by Permission

# WILL YOU LOVE ME TOMORROW

(Will You Still Love Me Tomorrow)

from BEAUTIFUL

HORN

Words and Music by GERRY GOFFIN
and CAROLE KING

Copyright © 1961 Screen Gems-EMI Music Inc.
Copyright Renewed
All Rights Administered by Sony/ATV Music Publishing LLC, 424 Church Street, Suite 1200, Nashville, TN 37219
International Copyright Secured All Rights Reserved

# WITH ONE LOOK

from SUNSET BOULEVARD

HORN

Music by ANDREW LLOYD WEBBER
Lyrics by DON BLACK and CHRISTOPHER HAMPTON,
with contributions by AMY POWERS

© Copyright 1993 Andrew Lloyd Webber licensed to The Really Useful Group Ltd.
International Copyright Secured All Rights Reserved

# WRITTEN IN THE STARS

from Elton John and Tim Rice's AIDA

HORN

Music by ELTON JOHN
Lyrics by TIM RICE

© 1999 Wonderland Music Company, Inc., Happenstance Ltd. and Evadon Ltd.
All Rights Reserved Used by Permission

# YOU RULE MY WORLD

from THE FULL MONTY

HORN

Words and Music by
DAVID YAZBEK

Copyright © 2000 Yeidlesounds Co., LLC (BMI)
Worldwide Rights for Yeidlesounds Co., LLC Administered by EMI Blackwood Music Inc.
All Rights Reserved Used by Permission

# YOU'LL NEVER WALK ALONE

from CAROUSEL

HORN

Lyrics by OSCAR HAMMERSTEIN II
Music by RICHARD RODGERS

Copyright © 1945 by Williamson Music, a Division of Rodgers & Hammerstein: an Imagem Company
Copyright Renewed
International Copyright Secured All Rights Reserved

# YOU'LL BE IN MY HEART

Disney Presents TARZAN The Broadway Musical

HORN

Words and Music by
PHIL COLLINS

© 1999 Edgar Rice Burroughs, Inc. and Walt Disney Music Company
All Rights Reserved Used by Permission

D.S. al Coda
CODA
1.
2.
3
3

# YOU'VE GOT A FRIEND

from BEAUTIFUL

HORN

Words and Music by
CAROLE KING

© 1971 (Renewed 1999) COLGEMS-EMI MUSIC INC.
All Rights Reserved International Copyright Secured Used by Permission

1.
Fine
2.
D.S. al Fine
(take 1st ending)

# YOUNGER THAN SPRINGTIME

from SOUTH PACIFIC

HORN

Lyrics by OSCAR HAMMERSTEIN II
Music by RICHARD RODGERS

**Moderately**

Copyright © 1949 by Richard Rodgers and Oscar Hammerstein II
Copyright Renewed
Williamson Music, a Division of Rodgers & Hammerstein: an Imagem Company, owner of publication and allied rights throughout the world
International Copyright Secured All Rights Reserved